AF207259

ISBN# 978-0-9985727-4-1

LEARNING VOCABULARY

THROUGH

Dialogue!

JUSTIN M. BUFFER

Created by Mr. Buffer, Founder and Director,
Cambridge Learning Center of NJ, MSE,
New Jersey Licensed Teacher

__What will this book help me with?__

This book will give you some great words to enrich your writing and give it a new level of sophistication. It will also help prepare you for many of the major assessments you will take in the future such as the SAT and the ACT, as well as giving you a jumpstart on some of the difficult material you will encounter in high school.

. . . .

Contents

<u>Writing Integration Word#1: Superfluous</u>

<u>Part of speech:</u> adjective

<u>Pronunciation:</u> so͞o ˈpərflo͞oəs

(Sup*er*-flow-us- emphasize the er)

Definition: unnecessary; beyond what is necessary, required, or sufficient

<u>Conversational/Dialogue Context Example:</u>

<u>Dad:</u> Priya, I want you to gather some of your old shirts that you don't wear anymore, and put them in a bag. We are going to donate them to charity.

<u>Priya</u>: Why dad? I have so many shirts and I love seeing them all lined up in my closet. I love having so many choices of what to wear.

<u>Dad:</u> Priya, the amount of shirts you have is **superfluous.** You only wear close to 20% of them, and the rest take up too much space in your closet! They are completely unnecessary. Let someone who really needs them have them.

<u>Writing Context Example:</u>

Frederica's mom knew that Frederica hated the cold weather, so she was not surprised when Frederica put on three layers of clothing before leaving the house. Her mother reminded her that it was only 51 degrees outside and that all she needed to wear was her sweater and her regular jacket. She told Frederica that she felt anything more than that was *superfluous* because it was not that cold out.

<u>Your Turn:</u>

A) Now, you use "superfluous" in a sentence of your own.

_____

_____

B) Now, you use "superfluous" in a paragraph of your own of 3-5 sentences:

_____

_____

_____

_____

_____

Writing Integration Word#2: Hubris

Part of speech: noun

Pronunciation: ˈ(h)yo͞obrəs

Definition: excessive pride or self-confidence

Conversational/Dialogue Context Example:

Ms. Baker is speaking with her students about an upcoming test. Nick, a student in her class, is explaining why he feels he does not have to study.

Ms. Baker: I want you all to study hard for the Geometry test on Friday. It will be very difficult and will be harder than any other test you have taken this school year.

Nick: I don't feel that I have to study that much because I really know it all so well. I think I can get a perfect score without even studying!

Ms. Baker: Nick, that seems like a very overconfident statement. I know you usually do well on tests, but this one will be in a different format. Last year, one of my students felt the same way and ended up not doing so well. If you don't study at all and don't take this seriously that will be a very extreme expression of **hubris**, and I think you will ultimately regret being so overconfident.

<u>Writing Context Example:</u>

One of the most common mistakes people who become very successful make is that they get overconfident and complacent and stop working hard. They feel that their success will never go away and that they can stop putting in as much effort as they used to. Such *hubris* can be very dangerous and harmful to people, ultimately leading to failure and loss of their success.

A) Now, you use "hubris" in a sentence of your own.

_____

_____

Your Turn:

Now, you use hubris in a paragraph of your own of 3-5 sentences:

_____

_____

_____

_____

_____

_____

Writing Integration Word#3: Frenetic

Part of speech: adjective

Pronunciation: frəˈnedik

Definition: Fast and energetic in a rather wild and uncontrolled way; filled with confusion; wild

Conversational/Dialogue Context Example:

Mom: Larry, I know your project is due in three weeks, after your break, but I want you to start it as soon as possible because I don't want you to do it at the last minute and feel rushed.

Larry: Mom, I understand, but I want to enjoy this holiday break, and I will start it in a week or so. I promise.

Mom: Larry, whenever you wait until the last minute to complete an assignment or project, or put things off, you get very anxious and end up doing everything, including your schoolwork, with a *frenetic* energy. I don't like seeing you this way and being this way negatively affects your grades. Whenever you are calm and unhurried, you clearly do much better.

<u>Writing Context Example:</u>

I hate to go shopping to the mall on very busy days because the atmosphere is extra *frenetic*. People are rushing into the stores, trying to get the best sales and prices. It feels like mayhem, especially at the busier department stores.

A) Now, you use "frenetic" in a sentence of your own.

_____

_____

Your Turn:

Now, you use "frenetic" in a paragraph of your own of 3-5 sentences:

_____

_____

_____

_____

_____

_____

Writing Integration Word#4: Mitigate

Part of speech: verb **Pronunciation:** midəˌgāt

Definition: To lessen the negative effects of; to make less severe, painful, or harmful

Conversational/Dialogue Context Example:

Mr. Breyer (Teacher): Class, I would like us all to come up with an idea together for a fundraiser and donation process to send money towards helping with world hunger. I want for each of you to brainstorm ideas for homework, and then we will have a class discussion about it tomorrow.

Barry (Student): Mr. Breyer, I am glad we will do this, but it seems so hopeless because no matter how much we do, we won't eliminate *all* of the hunger in the world. No matter how hard we try, there will still be people who are hungry and don't have enough to eat in the world.

Mr. Breyer (Teacher): Barry, of course, we cannot all by ourselves eliminate all suffering and maladies in the world. But, what we can do is *mitigate* this pain. Even if we can't help everyone, we can help someone in some way every day and lessen the adverse effects of hunger and other forms of suffering in the world.

<u>Writing Context Example:</u>

10-year old Ryan knew that every November he gets a cold. He gets a runny nose and experiences other symptoms, and then he knows that winter is surely here! He recently asked his family doctor, Dr. Sule, why something can't be invented to cure a common cold. She laughingly told him that there is no cure for the common cold and that we cannot cure it, but we can **mitigate** its effects with proper nutrition to boost our immune system and by taking our daily vitamins.

A) Now, you use "mitigate" in a sentence of your own.

_____

_____

Your Turn: Now, you use "mitigate" in a paragraph of your own of 3-5 sentences:

_____

_____

_____

_____

_____

Writing Integration Word#5: intractable

Part of speech: adjective

Pronunciation: ˌinˈtraktəb(ə)l

Definition#1 : Difficult to manage, deal with ,or to change to an acceptable behavior.

Definition#2 : Difficult to alleviate, remedy, or cure.

Conversational/Dialogue Context Example for definition:

Principal Smith: Ms. Lakota, what is happening with the students in your fifth period class? I hear a lot of noise coming from that room.

Ms. Lakota: Mr. Smith, two students in my class, Brad and Avery, are being very difficult. They will not stop calling out and are being very defiant. Then, when I have to stop teaching to speak with them, the rest of the class gets distracted and off course. I have tried everything with them, including taking away their classroom privileges, but they seem *intractable* now. So far, nothing has changed this unacceptable behavior.

Principal Smith: Have you tried yet to have a conference with their parents?

Ms. Lakota: That is my next step. I will be calling their homes tomorrow to set up a meeting with their parents.

<u>Writing Context Example:</u>

Abraham Lincoln's had some difficult days as President of the United States, especially related to the Civil War. He had to face the secession from the Union of many of the southern states that formed the Confederacy. He also had to deal with the death of his son, which was particularly painful for his wife. Also, the *intractable* stance of many of the Confederate leaders who refused to give up and surrender made fighting the war tough because he knew that he was overseeing a war that was literally tearing the country apart.

A) Now, you use "intractable" in a sentence of your own.

_____

_____

Your Turn:

Now, you use "intractable" in a paragraph of your own of 3-5 sentences:

_____

_____

_____

_____

_____

10

Writing Integration Word#6: quandary

Part of speech: noun

Pronunciation: kwän-d(ə-)rē\

Syllabic Breakdown: Kwan-da-ree

Definition: a difficult choice; a situation in which one feels confused about what to do

Synonyms:

Conversational/Dialogue Contextual Usage Example:

Selena: Ms. Smith, I was admitted to three Ivy League universities- Dartmouth, Yale, and Harvard! I am confused as to which one to go to.

Ms. Sarra (Guidance Counselor): Selena, wow that is quite a *quandary* you are immersed in! This situation is understandably a very hard choice and one that can affect the rest of your life, but you are fortunate to have such good choices! Many others would love to be in your shoes!

Selena: Yes it is a great quandary. Once I decide on this, though, my next quandary will be to major in law or medicine when I get to college!

<u>Writing Context Example:</u>

The governor of New York is running for President of the United States. He is excited about running for president but is facing a difficult *quandary* because he does not know whether he should remain Governor while he runs for president. He wants to make sure he gives his full time and best energy to running for president, but this very dedicated leader also wants to make sure the state is not neglected. All of these factors are making it a difficult choice. This difficult decision is going to take a few weeks to resolve as he assesses how much time running for president will require.

A) Now, you use "quandary" in a sentence of your own.

_____

_____

Your Turn:
Now, you use "quandary" in a paragraph of your own of 3-5 sentences:

_____

_____

_____

_____

_____

<u>Writing Integration Word#7: accentuate</u>

<u>Part of speech: verb</u>

<u>Pronunciation:</u> ək'sen(t)SHə͵wāt

<u>Definition:</u> to make something more noticeable; to empha-size; to make something "stand out" more.

<u>Conversational/Dialogue Contextual Usage Example:</u>

Jamie: Mark, I have noticed that Mrs. Nigel all of a sudden is underlining and bolding all the mistakes in my papers that are about commas and other punctuation more than she used to.

Mark: Yes, I have noticed the same thing. When I asked her why she does this now, she said it's because the state government announced that the statewide end-of-year exam this year would be very strict about punctuation us-age. So, she is trying to *accentuate* the importance of all of our commas, periods, and other relevant forms of punctua-tion by highlighting and bolding them with extra care. She wants to make sure we know how important it is to know this.

<u>Writing Context Example:</u>

Lonny noticed that his mother always liked to wear red-red shirts, red jackets, red lipstick, and more. When Lonny asked her about this, his mother said that her mother, Lonny's grandmother, had always told her that red *accentuates* her best features and makes her look her best.

A) Now, you use "accentuate" in a sentence of your own.

_____

_____

Your Turn: Now, you use "accentuate" in a paragraph of your own of 3-5 sentences:

_____

_____

_____

_____

_____

Writing Integration Word#8: malfeasance

Part of speech: noun

Pronunciation: mælˈfiz(ə)ns

Definition: wrongful conduct by a public official

Conversational/Dialogue Contextual Usage Example:

News Reporter (Questioning the Mayor): Mr. Mayor, how do you feel about the fact that your Assistant Mayor will go to prison for stealing money from the township?

Mayor: It is indeed very upsetting to me. Hopefully, this will be the last incident of **malfeasance** we will have amongst our local politicians and elected officials. Elected officials are chosen by the public, and they must take this trust very seriously. When they commit such wrongful acts, they violate the trust that the public has put in them.

Writing Context Example:

Many people do not trust politicians. I really cannot blame them because politicians so often do things that are illegal and use their power inappropriately. Such acts of *malfeasance* often make their way to the news on TV and into newspapers and make people not want to even follow politics or take them very seriously.

A)   Now, you use "malfeasance" in a sentence of your own.

_____

_____

Your Turn:

Now, you use "malfeasance" in a paragraph of your own of 3-5 sentences:

_____

_____

_____

_____

_____

Writing Integration Word#9: Truncated

Part of speech: adjective

Pronunciation: trəŋ-ˌkāted

Definition: shortened or reduced

Conversational/Dialogue Contextual Example:

Molly is at the library looking for a novel to read for her summer reading project

Molly: Excuse me Ms. Carter; I noticed this book I found in the teenage novel section seems to be a shorter version of a longer adult novel. Is that right?

Ms. Carter: (Librarian): Yes, Molly, you are correct. This book that you have here is a *truncated* version of the longer book. That's something that publishers sometimes do for children's books: they take a longer book and shorten it, making it more understandable and readable for young teenagers like yourself.

Molly: Oh, that's really good because I definitely don't want to read 500 pages! The *truncated* version works a lot better for me!

<u>Writing Context Example:</u>

On Monday morning, Martin had prepared a 30-minute speech to give on the PA system in school about why he should be elected president of the eighth grade. That morning, though, he was very surprised to hear the principal say that all of the candidates now had to keep their speeches under 10 minutes! This was because additional candidates had recently entered the race. So, Martin gave a *truncated* version of his prepared speech, leaving out parts that he felt were less important than others. Still, he thought he got his main message across and that he had done a pretty good job.

A) **Now, you use "truncated" in a sentence of your own.**

_____

_____

Your Turn:

Now, you use "truncated" in a paragraph of your own of 3-5 sentences:

_____

_____

_____

_____

_____

Other Usage examples of this word you should know

Truncate (Verb): *President Obama worked on his State of the Union speech at the White House for three days straight. When realizing that his speech was too long, he decided to **truncate** it and cut it down by one hour.*

Writing Integration Word#10: Panacea

Part of speech: noun

Pronunciation: pa-no-ˈsee-ə

Definition: a remedy for all ills or difficulties; a cure all

Conversational/Dialogue Contextual Example:

** Brian is having a conversation with his mother who wants him to eat more vegetables. **

Bryan's Mom: Bryan, I know you remember I told you that I want you to eat more vegetables. There are too many vegetables left on your plate, and I told you how important they are for you!

Bryan: I know they are important, Mom, but you told me that they would help me keep me healthy and provide important nutrients. But then why the other day did I still get a cold and a fever, even though I've been eating so many vegetables lately?

Bryan's Mom: Bryan, I didn't say that vegetables were a *panacea* and that they would take care of every illness, or every problem you have or will have! My main point, Bryan, is that that they are important and for the long-term will play an important part in keeping you healthy, along with exercise, a positive attitude, and good, everyday hygiene.

Writing Context Example:

There are groups of people in the world who want to help bring world peace for the long term. One of the most popular ideas they have is to form summer camps where children from different countries that have for many years been enemies can come together and learn more about each other. These children learn that, despite the differences in their native countries' histories and the fact that their ancestors fought for many years, they have a lot in common as human beings.

Although the creators of these camps know that these camps will not be a *panacea* for all the world's conflicts, wars, and fighting, and they know that these camps will not magically create world peace; they do feel that they will help just a little bit and help make a difference for the long-term

A) Now, you use "panacea" in a sentence of your own.

_____

_____

Your Turn:

Now, you use "panacea" in a paragraph of your own of 3-5 sentences:

_____

_____

_____

_____

_____

_____

Writing Integration Word#11: amalgam

Part of speech: noun

Pronunciation: ə-ˈmal-gem

Syllabic Breakdown: am-al-gam

Definition: a combination of two or more things

Conversational/Dialogue Contextual

Usage Example:

*** Karen and Bridgett are having a conversation about Bridgett's favorite restaurant ***

Karen: Bridgett, I know that you go to Luigi's Café for dinner often. I have never been there, but I am sure if you go there so often that it is a very good restaurant!

Bridgett: Yes, it is indeed such a good and unique restaurant. My husband and I love going there.

Karen: Really, what is so special about it?

Bridgett: It has everything that we like. It is the perfect *amalgam* of great food, great music, and great fun. It is hard to find a restaurant with all three of these characteristics. Most restaurants we have tried only have one of these qualities, which are all important to me when I choose a restaurant.

<u>Writing Context Example:</u>

Chad was very disappointed when he heard from his father this morning that the concert for his favorite band The Bugs was canceled at the Garden State Arts Center. He did not understand why the stadium chose to cancel it, and his father didn't have the exact reason just yet. When Chad researched on the Internet for answers, he realized it was a ***amalgam*** of factors that caused the cancelation of the concert: the impending snow storm, the fact that the lead singer of the band was sick, and the fact that the road leading into the stadium was closed because of flooding. All these factors together explained why the concert was canceled.

A) Now, you use "amalgam" in a sentence of your own.

_____

_____

Your Turn:

Now, you use "amalgam" in a paragraph of your own of 3-5 sentences:

_____

_____

_____

_____

_____

_____

<u>Other Usages for and information about amalgam</u>

<u>Amalgam (Noun):</u> When mercury is combined with other metals it is called an amalgam. This combination was often used as a dental filling for a long time throughout history.

Source: Ferracane, Jack L. (2001). *Materials in Dentistry: Principles and Applications.* Lippincott Williams & Wilkins. p. 3.

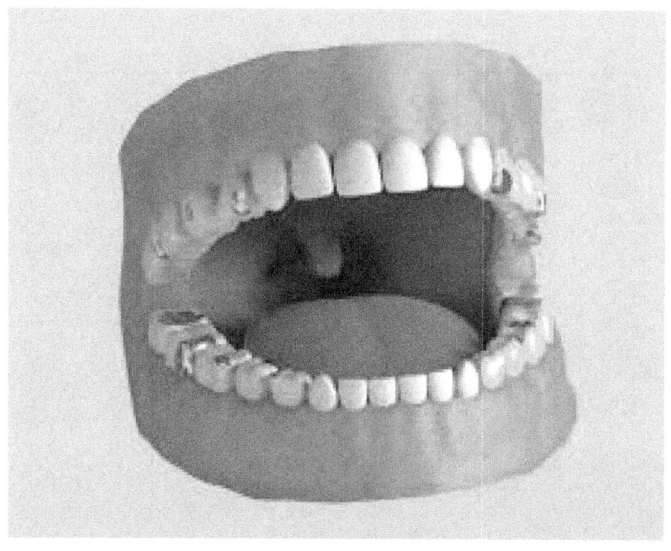

Writing Integration Word#12: lucid

Part of speech: adjective

Pronunciation: \ˈlü-səd\

Definition: very clear and easy to understand

Conversational/Dialogue Contextual Usage Example:

Mr. Baker (John's father): John, who is your favorite teacher in school?

John: Dad, my favorite teacher is my Science teacher, Mrs. Carter. Her explanations are so good, and they help me to understand everything so well.

Mr. Baker: That is great to hear. What are some of the more difficult concepts that her teaching helped you to understand?

John: Cellular respiration! I did not understand it at first, but she was so good at making it so clear for me!

Mr. Baker: Wow, that is great ! When I was your age, I also liked teachers whose explanations were so **lucid**. The teachers who make things easier for us to understand are usually the teachers we remember.

Writing Context Usage Example:

A) Now, you use "lucid" in a sentence of your own.

_____

_____

Your Turn: Now, you use "lucid" in a paragraph of your own of 3-5 sentences:

_____

_____

_____

_____

_____

_____

28

Writing Integration Word#13: Abate

Part of speech: Noun

Pronunciation: /əˈbeɪt/

Definition: To decrease in intensity, degree or quantity; to lessen or diminish

Related Usages: Abated (past tense form)

Conversational/Dialogue Context Example:

Sue: If the rain continues, I will have to go home in the rain. Thankfully, I came with an umbrella. It was as if I knew I would need the umbrella.

Janice: You are lucky. I forgot my umbrella at home. I will have to wait for the rain to **abate** before I leave here.

Writing Context Example:

The price of oil is expected to continue to rise. This is due to the conflict between oil-producing countries. Only something very drastic like a ceasefire can make the rise in oil prices *abate*.

<u>Your Turn:</u>

A) Now, you use "abate" in a sentence of your own.

_____

_____

B) Now, you use "abate" in a paragraph of your own of 3-5 sentences:

_____

_____

_____

_____

_____

_____

Writing Integration Word#14: Abdicate

Part of speech: Noun

Pronunciation: /ˈæb.də.keɪt/

Definition: To fail to undertake; renouncing your duty, throne or dignity; discard

Related Usages: Abdicated (Past tense),

Conversational/Dialogue Context Example:

Professor Kent and David his student are talking about the government's economic policy.

Professor Kent: I believe the government's effort to encourage private sector investment in healthcare is counterproductive.

David (student): In my opinion, outsourcing healthcare management is a brilliant move. It will usher in efficiency and attract the best hands into the healthcare sector.

Professor Kent: I am not yet convinced. I think these are all excuses given by the government to **abdicate** its responsibilities.

<u>Writing Context Example:</u>

The protests in the capital city continued. It's been a month since the protests began and the protestors have only one demand: They want the president to resign. They accuse him of ruining the economy and junketing around the world. They want a leader that will not *abdicate* his responsibilities in search of pleasure.

<u>Your Turn:</u>

A) Now, you use "abdicate" in a sentence of your own.

_____

_____

B) Now, you use "abdicate" in a paragraph of your own of 3-5 sentences:

_____

_____

_____

_____

_____

Writing Integration Word#15: Brazen

Part of speech: Adjective

Pronunciation: /ˈbreɪz(ə)n/

Definition: Boldness without shame

Related Usages: Brazenly (Adverb)

Conversational/Dialogue Context Example:

Pedro: Have you read Miguel's article on his involvement in the case of fraud?

Ian: I did. It is a shame he still attempted to exonerate himself after being convicted on all charges brought against him.

Pedro: I was surprised at his **brazen** attempt to make it seem as though he was being falsely accused.

Writing Context Example:

It's unnecessary getting angry with Adams. Adams has a poor attitude and is known for displaying a ***brazen*** disregard for other people's feelings. A lot of people don't like him at the office.

<u>Your Turn:</u>

A) Now, you use "brazen" in a sentence of your own.

_____

_____

B) Now, you use "brazen" in a paragraph of your own of 3-5 sentences:

_____

_____

_____

_____

_____

_____

Writing Integration Word#16: Capacious

Part of speech: Adjective

Pronunciation: /kəˈpeɪʃəs/

Definition: Having a lot of space; Roomy, Spacious

Conversational/Dialogue Context Example:

Sara an architect is presenting building plans she has prepared to Carmen her client.

Sara (Architect): Here are the building plans. I have designed the exterior of the building to reflect your love for modern art. The walls are fitted with art pieces you will love.

Carmen (Client): That is lovely. Tell me about the interior of the building.

Sara (Architect): The interior of the building sports a minimalist design with **capacious** rooms that reflect an artistic use of space. I am sure you'll find the spacious rooms a welcome change from the cramped apartments you complained about.

Writing Context Example:

Amanda and her husband wanted to get a new car but all the options the car dealer offered them did not match what they wanted. They wanted a car with enough legroom and a *capacious* trunk so they could take their luggage when going on a trip.

Your Turn:

A) Now, you use "capacious" in a sentence of your own.

_____

_____

B) Now, you use "capacious" in a paragraph of your own of 3-5 sentences:

_____

_____

_____

_____

_____

<u>Writing Integration Word#17: Capitulate</u>

Part of speech: Verb

Pronunciation: /kəˈpɪtjʊleɪt/

Definition: To cease to resist an opponent; to give in or yield to a demand

Related Usages: Capitulated (Past Tense)

<u>Conversational/Dialogue Context Example:</u>

Eva and Janice are both moms. Eva is telling her about her son Derrick and his love for action figures.

Eva: Derrick is growing so fast that I sometimes struggle to keep up. He is so full of energy!

Janice: Kids are like that. They grow very fast. It was just like yesterday when he was a tiny infant. I am sure he's already asking for train sets.

Eva: Derrick loves action figures. I promised to get him a few for Christmas. However, Derrick persistently asks me to get them before Christmas. I fear I will **capitulate** soon and get him the action figures.

Writing Context Example:

In a bid to avoid civil unrest and a general strike, the government was forced to *capitulate* to the union's demands for a new wage structure. Negotiations on the new wage structure will begin next week. The unions believe this is a noteworthy victory.

Your Turn:

A) Now, you use "capitulate" in a sentence of your own.

_____

_____

B) Now, you use "capitulate" in a paragraph of your own of 3-5 sentences:

_____

_____

_____

_____

_____

_____

Writing Integration Word#18: Condescending

Part of speech: Adjective

Pronunciation: /kɒndɪˈsɛndɪŋ/

Definition: To show an attitude that indicates superiority; patronizing

Related Usages: condescend (verb)

Conversational/Dialogue Context Example:

Brian comes out of a meeting looking upset. The following conversation ensues between him and Audrey his assistant at the office.

Audrey: How did the meeting go? You look upset.

Brian: I don't think the meeting went well. The investors do not believe we are equal partners in this merger.

Audrey: What are their demands?

Brian: They are requesting that in the event of a merger, we replace our line managers with persons from their firm. I find that a **condescending** request.

<u>Writing Context Example:</u>

Freda is a pretty young banker. She is very intelligent, has a great smile, and does a terrific job at the office. Freda posts great results and meets all her targets every year for the company. The bosses love her because she gets the job done. Her subordinates at work, however, find her a bit *condescending* in the way she relates with them.

<u>Your Turn:</u>

A) Now, you use "condescending" in a sentence of your own.

_____

_____

B) Now, you use "condescending" in a paragraph of your own of 3-5 sentences:

_____

_____

_____

_____

_____

_____

Writing Integration Word#19: Convergence

Part of speech: Noun

Pronunciation: \ kən-ˈvər-jəns\

Definition: Merging of different entities into a unified whole

Related Usages: Convergent (adjective)

Conversational/Dialogue Context Example:

Ken and Mary are discussing after a presentation Susan and Mary made in class

Ken: I like the format you came up with for your presentation in which the advantages of the new law are presented before the disadvantages. It brings to the fore the positives of the law.

Mary: That was Susan's idea. She brought the suggestion of discussing the new law with more emphasis on the advantages.

Ken: I also loved the way you made references to similar laws in other South American countries.

Mary: Thank you. This presentation is a convergence of Susan's ideas and my ideas. I am glad it turned out well.

<u>Writing Context Example:</u>

There's hardly heavy traffic during the day or at midday on 9th street. However, when heavy traffic occurs, it is usually due to the ***convergence*** of different factors. It is either there is an event at the nearby City Hall or a game at the stadium.

<u>Your Turn:</u>

A) Now, you use "convergence" in a sentence of your own.

_____

_____

B) Now, you use "convergence" in a paragraph of your own of 3-5 sentences:

_____

_____

_____

_____

_____

_____

Writing Integration Word#20: deleterious

Part of speech: Adjective (formal)

Pronunciation: /ˌdɛlɪˈtɪərɪəs/

Definition: instigating damage or harmful

Conversational/Dialogue Context Example:

Elsie who just returned from a trip abroad as a volunteer is sharing her experience with her friends Kendra and Toby

Toby: How did you spend your time as a volunteer? Whatever you did must have been fun and engaging.

Elsie: It was a lot more tiring than it was fun but I enjoyed every bit of it. As a volunteer, I helped organize the distribution of relief materials to the people in need. I also spent time helping out at the school in the refugee camp.

Kendra: That is awesome. I'm sure the children all loved you.

Elsie: I think they did. The war had a **deleterious** effect on the children. I wish I met them under better circumstances.

<u>Writing Context Example:</u>

Research has shown that the consistent consumption of drugs has a *deleterious* effect on human health. This research is not limited to hard drugs. Even continued exposure to prescribed drugs has been known to have such deleterious effects as well.

<u>Your Turn:</u>

A) Now, you use "deleterious" in a sentence of your own.

_____

_____

B) Now, you use "deleterious" in a paragraph of your own of 3-5 sentences:

_____

_____

_____

_____

_____

_____

Writing Integration Word#21: Diligent

Part of speech: Adjective

Pronunciation: /ˈdɪlɪdʒ(ə)nt/

Definition: Involving a lot of care and effort

Related Usages: Diligence (Noun)

Conversational/Dialogue Context Example:

Sanchez and Freddie are talking about Jeff who just got a scholarship

Sanchez: I just spoke with Jeff on the phone. He told me he was awarded a scholarship.

Freddie: This is great news! I am glad he got this. I think he deserves this; he had been working hard for a long time towards clinching the scholarship.

Sanchez: Jeff has been **diligent** in his studies. He has also been consistent as an athlete. I agree that he deserves the scholarship.

<u>Writing Context Example:</u>

Graduating from high school and getting a scholarship takes great effort. Hence, students are often advised to be *diligent* in their academic pursuits. Students who do well in school find it easier to get academic scholarships than students who perform poorly academically.

<u>Your Turn:</u>

A) Now, you use "diligent" in a sentence of your own.

_____

_____

B) Now, you use "diligent" in a paragraph of your own of 3-5 sentences:

_____

_____

_____

_____

_____

Writing Integration Word#22: Emulate

Part of speech: Verb

Pronunciation: /ˈem.jə.leɪt/

Definition: Matching or surpassing the feats of someone great by imitation

Related Usages: Emulated (Past tense)

Conversational/Dialogue Context Example:

Ahmed and Josh are talking about historical characters after a visit to the museum

Josh: My favorite historical figure is Thomas Edison. He inspires me to keep on trying until I succeed.

Ahmed: I don't think I have a favorite historical figure.

Josh: There's got to be a historical figure who you would want to be like. Someone you hope to **emulate**.

Ahmed: In that case, I'd say my favorite person in history is Leonardo da Vinci. He was skilled in many fields of knowledge.

<u>Writing Context Example:</u>

Paul is a great dad. He has three kids. Before his first child was born, he used to smoke cigarettes. He quit smoking after his first child was born because he didn't want his kids to watch and *emulate* his smoking habit.

<u>Your Turn:</u>

A) Now, you use "emulate" in a sentence of your own.

_____

_____

B) Now, you use "emulate" in a paragraph of your own of 3-5 sentences:

_____

_____

_____

_____

_____

_____

Writing Integration Word#23: Enervating

Part of speech: Verb

Pronunciation: /ˈɛnəveɪt/

Definition: To make weak and lack energy

Conversational/Dialogue Context Example:

It is summer and Sonia and Vena are outdoors doing some gardening

Vena: The pace of work today is very slow Sonia. I don't understand why I am slow today. I usually apply manure to the whole garden within shorter periods.

Sonia: I think the weather is contributing to this. It is hot and the temperature is getting close to thirty degrees Celsius. The *enervating* heat is responsible for our sluggish pace of work.

Writing Context Example:

Going through surgery can be a painful experience. Surgery can be very *enervating* and the pain can go on for weeks. At this point, you may need to be administered energy-giving supplements.

<u>Your Turn:</u>

A) Now, you use "enervating" in a sentence of your own.

_____

_____

B) Now, you use "enervating" in a paragraph of your own of 3-5 sentences:

_____

_____

_____

_____

_____

_____

Writing Integration Word#24: Ephemeral

Part of speech: Adjective

Pronunciation: /ɪˈfem.ər.əl/

Definition 1: Lasting for a short time or briefly

Conversational/Dialogue Context Example:

Jane and Joe just returned from a holiday in the Bahamas. They run into their friend Graham at the mall.

Graham: Hi guys. It is good to see you. When did you return?

Jane: We got back on Wednesday.

Graham: That is lovely. I guess you had a good time in the Bahamas.

Joe: We sure did. It was an **ephemeral** vacation. We just spent 10 days there. We hope to visit there again and spend more time there.

Writing Context Example:

Love is a beautiful thing. It's one of the best things that can happen to anyone. Love, rather being *ephemeral* should be a lifetime commitment. You don't get to experience the beauty of love if it's momentary.

<u>Your Turn:</u>

A) Now, you use "ephemeral" in a sentence of your own.

_____

_____

B) Now, you use "ephemeral" in a paragraph of your own of 3-5 sentences:

_____

_____

_____

_____

_____

_____

Writing Integration Word#25: Florid

Part of speech: Adjective

Pronunciation: /ˈflɒrɪd/

Definition 1: Having excessive intricate decorations and details

Definition 2: Having a red complexion

Related Usages: Floridly (adverb)

Conversational/Dialogue Context Example:

Constantine a tour guide is describing a building to a tour group (of which James is a member).

James: That is a lovely building. Look at the intricate carvings on the walls!

Constantine: This church dates back to the 15th century. It is said that it took over 15 years to complete the construction of the church.

James: I would not doubt that. The **florid** carvings on the walls of the building would take a lot of time to complete.

Constantine: It might interest you to know that there are over 17,000 carved figures on the walls.

<u>Conversational/Dialogue Context Example 2:</u>

Jasmine and Christina meet at the beauty salon

Jasmine: Hi Christina, it is so good to see you. I never knew you came here.

Christina: I only started coming here recently. I heard they offer the best skincare treatments.

Jasmine: They do. Samantha is my favorite skincare specialist here. She does such a great job whenever she attends to me.

Christina: I don't think I have met Samantha.

Jasmine: I am sure you have. Samantha is quite popular here. She has blonde hair and is **florid.**

<u>Writing Context Example:</u>

Jane is a very timid girl. Her father came visiting her in college. As she came over to meet him she tripped and fell on the steps of the library. She was very embarrassed and her face went **florid** immediately.

<u>Your Turn:</u>

A) Now, you use "florid" in a sentence of your own.

_____

_____

B) Now, you use "florid" in a paragraph of your own of 3-5 sentences:

_____

_____

_____

_____

_____

_____

Writing Integration Word#26: Fortuitous

Part of speech: Adjective

Pronunciation: /fɔːˈtjuːɪtəs/

[fawr-too-i-tuhs]

Definition: Occurring by chance

Related Usages: Fortuitously (Adverb)

Conversational/Dialogue Context Example:

Linda just won a quiz competition. Sandra comes over to congratulations.

Sandra: Congratulations Linda. Your performance blew my mind. I was on the edge of my seat all through the event.

Linda: Thanks, Sandra. It was an intense experience for me as well. I was quite nervous too.

Sandra: How did you know the answers to all the questions? I was awed when you gave the correct answer to the question requesting the number of provinces in Serbia. How could you have known?

Linda: I did not know all the answers to the questions. My answer to the question on the number of provinces in Serbia was **fortuitous**. I was surprised it turned out to be correct.

Writing Context Example:

Vera had an interview one Monday morning, but she woke up late. She had already missed the bus and the next bus was coming in 30 minutes. It seemed there was no way she would make it to the interview. Fortunately for her, she ran into James her classmate who was driving his dad to work in the same building where the interview was to be held. James asked her to join them in the car and took her to her interview. Vera even-tually got the job. She always looks back to her *fortuitous* meeting with James on the day of her interview.

Your Turn:

A) Now, you use "fortuitous" in a sentence of your own.

_____

_____

B) Now, you use "fortuitous" in a paragraph of your own of 3-5 sentences:

_____

_____

_____

_____

_____

Writing Integration Word#27: Foster

Part of speech: Verb

Pronunciation: /ˈfɒstə/

Definition: To encourage the growth of something

Definition 2: To raise a child that is not one's own by birth

Related Usages: Fostered (Past tense)

Conversational/Dialogue Context Example:

It is campaign season and Peter a gubernatorial candidate is granting Sally an interview.

Sally: Looking at your manifesto there are several programs you hope to implement if you win. What do you hope to achieve with these programs?

Peter: Thank you, Sally. When you look at these programs closely, they are all designed to improve the living standards of the people in the state. We hope to ensure that the little economic growth we are experiencing is nurtured. In a nutshell, what we hope to do with these programs is to **foster** economic growth and improve living standards.

Conversational/Dialogue Context Example 2:

David and Michelle Robin are visiting an orphanage. They meet with Mrs. Greystone who is the director.

Mrs. Greystone: Thank you for visiting us, Mr. and Mrs. Robin. We are always happy to receive visitors. What are your intentions?

David: I am happy to be here as well. My wife and I have decided to adopt a child and we were hoping you could guide us on how to go about it.

Michelle: We would be happy to **foster** a child and provide a loving family for her to grow in.

Mrs. Greystone: I am pleased to hear this. We will run the necessary background checks and begin the official adoption process next week.

<u>Writing Context Example: Foster.</u>

Crime rates easily rise in slums and places where people live in unhealthy conditions devoid of government attention. Conditions such as these *foster* the growth of crime rates. The authorities must ensure that the standard of living is improved.

<u>Your Turn:</u>

A) Now, you use "foster" in a sentence of your own.

_____

_____

B) Now, you use "foster" in a paragraph of your own of 3-5 sentences:

_____

_____

_____

_____

_____

_____

Writing Integration Word#28: Impetuous

Part of speech: Adjective

Pronunciation: /ɪmˈpɛtjʊəs/

Definition: Acting without care or thought; acting carelessly and swiftly

Related Usages: Impetuously (Adverb)

Conversational/Dialogue Context Example:

It is fresher's orientation, Adam and Jack are discussing the clubs they signed up for.

Adam: How many clubs did you sign up for? I signed up with the badminton club, the French society, and the culinary society.

Jack: I signed up for about nine clubs. I signed up with the French society, the Spanish club, the AI club, Toastmasters, Swimming Club, African Club, and the Historical Society.

Adam: How do you intend to cope with all of these? Have you thought this through? I have a feeling your decision to join all these clubs is an impetuous decision.

<u>Writing Context Example:</u>

Tony has stuck with the belief that Collins is an *impetuous* young man. This is because Tony doesn't care about his appearance and rarely shaves his beards. Tony and Collins always argue about his appearance whenever they meet. Collins, however, has remained adamant and believes his appearance has no bearing with his personality.

<u>Your Turn:</u>

A) Now, you use "impetuous" in a sentence of your own.

_____

_____

B) Now, you use "impetuous" in a paragraph of your own of 3-5 sentences:

_____

_____

_____

_____

_____

Writing Integration Word#29: Intrepid

Part of speech: Adjective

Pronunciation: /ɪnˈtrɛpɪd/

Definition: Being fearless, brave and resolute

Conversational/Dialogue Context Example:

Jonas is telling Matteo about the weekend when he went kayaking, hiking and rock climbing

Jonas: Last weekend was probably the most remarkable weekend of my life. I went camping, rock climbing, and hiking. Kendrick was there too.

Matteo: Kendrick lives for things like these. He loves the outdoors and spends most of his free time outdoors.

Jonas: This makes sense. Kendrick is a brave and fearless person and his **intrepid** nature came to the fore in all the activities we engaged in. He was the only person who went Kayaking in the rushing waters of the rapids when everyone else was scared to.

<u>Writing Context Example:</u>

It's common for some people to brag about their brave feats. However, truly *intrepid* people rarely talk about their feats; they let other people tell of their bravery. They'd rather show by action their bravery than regale people with stories of their bravery.

<u>Your Turn:</u>

A) Now, you use "intrepid" in a sentence of your own.

_____

_____

B) Now, you use "intrepid" in a paragraph of your own of 3-5 sentences:

_____

_____

_____

_____

_____

Writing Integration Word#30: Jubilation

Part of speech: Noun

Pronunciation: /dʒuːbɪˈleɪʃn/

Definition: Feeling of great happiness, triumph, and celebration

Related Usages: Jubilant (adjective)

Conversational/Dialogue Context Example:

Brazil wins the FIFA world cup and Eva calls her brother Tim who works in Brazil to chat.

Eva: Congratulations, Tim! Brazil has won the world cup just as you said they would. How is the atmosphere over there?

Tim: The atmosphere is like a carnival. Cars are honking on the streets, people are dancing and celebrating everywhere. I am sure the **jubilation** will continue until late in the night. Everybody is very happy with this major triumph.

<u>Writing Context Example:</u>

The end of the year is characterized by heartfelt joy. At the Thanksgiving dinner which every member of the family looks forward to, there's an abundance of *jubilation.* Everyone is happy to be home.

<u>Your Turn:</u>

A) Now, you use "jubilation" in a sentence of your own.

_____

_____

B) Now, you use "jubilation" in a paragraph of your own of 3-5 sentences:

_____

_____

_____

_____

_____

_____

Writing Integration Word#31: Prosaic

Part of speech: Adjective

Pronunciation: /prə(ʊ)ˈzeɪɪk/

Definition 1: Using the writing style of prose as opposed to poetry

Definition 2: Commonplace and unromantic

Conversational/Dialogue Context Example:

Kevin sees Vivian with a book at the café and the following conversation follows.

Kevin: Hi Vivian. What book is that? It looks like an interesting book from the cover.

Vivian: You know what they say about judging books by their covers. However, this is an interesting book. It is by Sam Baldwin and the title is The Mourning Water Lily.

Kevin: I like Sam Baldwin, but I prefer books by his broth-er Ethan. Ethan Baldwin's books have strong poetic influ-ence and I love poetry. Sam Baldwin is a prosaic writer in my opinion.

Vivian: Well, you are a poet so your preference is understandable.

Conversational/Dialogue Context Example 2:

Jessica returns home from a date with Lee. She tells her roommate Tess about the date

Tess: You are back quite early. How did your first date with Lee go?

Jessica: It went well but I did not enjoy it. We met at the mall and it was crowded and noisy because of the holiday shoppers. For our next date, I will suggest a less crowded place.

Tess: A mall seems like a **prosaic** choice for a date. I know a site that has awesome suggestions for first dates. You can look it up before your next date.

Writing Context Example:

Maris is a writer. She writes romance novels and short stories. Her style is engaging and fun. She loves attaching emotions to her writing so that her readers can enjoy every piece of it. She strives to avoid being a *prosaic* writer.

Your Turn:

A) Now, you use "prosaic" in a sentence of your own.

_____

_____

B) Now, you use "prosaic" in a paragraph of your own of 3-5 sentences:

_____

_____

_____

_____

_____

_____

Writing Integration Word#32: Provocative

Part of speech: Adjective

Pronunciation: /prəˈvɒkətɪv/

Definition 1: Deliberately causing a strong reaction, especially anger.

Definition 2: Intended to elicit sexual desire or interest

Conversational/Dialogue Context Example:

Marvin and Melinda are discussing an article they had just read online

Marvin: This is completely false. How could the author make such wild claims without evidence to back it up? I am beginning to get angry.

Melinda: This is what he set out to do from the start. I believe the article was written to get readers angry and start writing rejoinders. That way the issue of the demolitions will be brought back to the fore of the public discussion.

Marvin: There are better ways to do that than writing **provocative** newspaper articles.

Conversational/Dialogue Context Example 2:

Keisha who is preparing for an interview is asking Liz for advice.

Keisha: What forms of dressing are ideal for a job interview? This is my first interview and I want to get everything right.

Liz: You just need to appear formal as though you were coming for a business meeting. You'll be fine.

Keisha: Thank you very much.

Liz: You should also note that dresses with plunging necklines are considered **provocative** in many workspaces.

Writing Context Example:

The governor has apologized for his comments at the gala. He explained that he was hurt by the **provocative** accusations the protesters made against him. He agreed, however, that he was wrong to have lashed out at them the way he did.

Your Turn:

A) **Now, you use "provocative" in a sentence of your own.**

_____

_____

B) Now, you use "provocative" in a paragraph of your own of 3-5 sentences:

Writing Integration Word#33: Prudent

Part of speech: Adjective

Pronunciation: /ˈpruːd(ə)nt/

Definition: Acting carefully and sensibly and avoiding unnecessary risks

Related Usages: Prudently (Adverb)

Conversational/Dialogue Context Example:

Vince and Williams who are coworkers are talking about happenings in their company.

Vince: The latest figures from sales indicate that our profits have grown by 21%. The sales manager also announced that we are expanding into three new countries next year.

Williams: The credit for all these should go to the CEO. Since he was appointed to head the company, the company has been growing in leaps and bounds. He turned the company from a liability to a profit-making company in three years.

Vince: The CEO is a **prudent** man who always thinks carefully before making any decision. He always seeks staff input before making any major decisions. I am sure we will even make more profit next year.

<u>Writing Context Example:</u>

With the president's **prudent** management of the economy, it is expected that the economy will exit recession and enter into a phase of growth. Already there are signs of growth in the industrial sector. So far over 200,000 jobs have been added in the sector and more are expected to come before the year ends.

<u>Your Turn:</u>

A) Now, you use "prudent" in a sentence of your own.

_____

_____

B) Now, you use "prudent" in a paragraph of your own of 3-5 sentences:

_____

_____

_____

_____

_____

Writing Integration Word#34: Rancorous

Part of speech: Adjective

Pronunciation: /ˈraŋk(ə)rəs/

Definition: Full of bitterness, resentment, and anger

Conversational/Dialogue Context Example:

Mrs. Jones attempts to pacify Wendy who just stormed out of a meeting with her band.

Mrs. Jones: Wendy, please calm down and have a cup of water. I can see the meeting did not go very well.

Wendy: The meeting was terrible. It was **rancorous**. It is probably the worst meeting of my entire life. I do not understand why everyone was angry and bitter at me. It was like they all blamed me squarely for our failures this year!

Mrs. Jones: There is not much we can achieve in a **rancorous** atmosphere. I think you should hold another meeting when everyone is less angry.

<u>Writing Context Example:</u>

In an organization, where members go against the plan or fail to obey rules, there are bound to be **rancorous** disputes. It is not a surprise that the young record label is experiencing these storms. The members of the management team did not obey the rules they set up.

<u>Your Turn:</u>

A) Now, you use "rancorous" in a sentence of your own.

_____

_____

B) Now, you use "rancorous" in a paragraph of your own of 3-5 sentences:

_____

_____

_____

_____

_____

Writing Integration Word#35: Reclusive

Part of speech: Adjective

Pronunciation: /rɪˈkluːsɪv/

Definition: Living by avoiding the company of other people; solitary

Related Usages: Recluse (Noun)

Conversational/Dialogue Context Example:

Ivan: I just met Mr. Winterbottom out on the streets. Do you know that Mr. Winterbottom is a Billionaire? He is so humble and unassuming.

Salim: I do not even know who Mr. Winterbottom is. Who is he and what does he do for a living?

Ivan: Many people do not know of him because he is a **reclusive** man. He lives shielded away from the eyes of the public on his private island. He rarely speaks to the press and he is not a fan of social media. He made his money during the dotcom boom and has lived a **reclusive** lifestyle ever since.

<u>Writing Context Example:</u>

Many people did not have an idea of how the crown prince would rule the kingdom. He had been a **reclusive** person for most of his adult life and only a few people knew what he was like personally. It is hoped that after his appointment as the crown prince he would have more interactions with the public.

<u>Your Turn:</u>

A) Now, you use "reclusive" in a sentence of your own.

_____

_____

B) Now, you use "reclusive" in a paragraph of your own of 3-5 sentences:

_____

_____

_____

_____

_____

Writing Integration Word#36: Sagacity

Part of speech: Noun

Pronunciation: /səˈgasɪti/

Definition: Having the quality of being discerning and wise

Conversational/Dialogue Context Example:

Silvia: There are sirens, flashing lights and police squad cars in the neighborhood. I wonder what is going on.

Dan: There was a reporter on the news this evening saying the police had arrested the suspected masterminds behind the bank heist that happened on North Street 5 years ago.

Silvia: If that is true then the police must have displayed a rare level of **sagacity**. The case had been under investigation for over 4 years and it appeared as if it was impossible to crack.

Writing Context Example:

Our new IT manager at work is very good at what he does. He is an engineer of surprising **sagacity** considering he just got the job and has little experience. He has done well for himself despite his young age.

<u>Your Turn:</u>

A) Now, you use "sagacity" in a sentence of your own.

_____

_____

B) Now, you use "sagacity" in a paragraph of your own of 3-5 sentences:

_____

_____

_____

_____

_____

_____

Writing Integration Word#37: Vindicate

Part of speech: Verb

Pronunciation: ˈvɪndɪkeɪt/

Definition 1: to justify, prove right, reinforce an idea

Definition 2: to absolve from guilt

Related Usages: Vindication (noun)

Conversational/Dialogue Context Example 1:

Karen: I had always said that the best way to grow profit is to lower our prices to reach more customers.

Ashley: I am glad the manager listened to you. The sales records they posted yesterday vindicate you.

Conversational/Dialogue Context Example 2:

Karen: What did the judge say about the woman who was accused of fraud?

Ashley: The judge said that the prosecution did not have enough evidence to show she was guilty of fraud.

Karen: The woman had constantly maintained that she was innocent. She fingered her nephew as the person who committed the fraud using her credit card.

Ashley: The testimony a special investigator gave was what was used by her lawyers to vindicate her. I'm glad she is now free to go home to her family.

<u>Writing Context Example:</u>

Sarah was taken to court on charges of money laundering. She had always maintained that she was innocent. During the trial, an external auditor testified. The external auditor's testimony was used by her lawyers to **vindicate** her in court.

<u>Your Turn:</u>

A) **Now, you use "vindicate" in a sentence of your own.**

_____

_____

B) **Now, you use "vindicate" in a paragraph of your own of 3-5 sentences:**

_____

_____

_____

_____

_____

_____

Made in the USA
Middletown, DE
05 November 2023

41822625R00050